Let's Celebrate America

Fort McHenry

Our Flag was Still There

by Joanne Mattern

Let's Celebrate America is produced and published by Red Chair Press:
Red Chair Press LLC PO Box 333 South Egremont, MA 01258-0333
www.redchairpress.com

About the Author

Joanne Mattern is a former editor and the author of nearly 350 books for children and teens. She began writing when she was a little girl and just never stopped! Joanne loves nonfiction because she enjoys bringing history and science topics to life and showing young readers that nonfiction is full of compelling stories! Joanne lives in New York State with her husband, four children, and several pets.

Publisher's Cataloging-In-Publication Data
Names: Mattern, Joanne, 1963–
Title: Fort McHenry : our flag was still there / by Joanne Mattern.

Description: South Egremont, MA : Red Chair Press, [2017] | Series: Let's celebrate America | Interest age level: 008-012. | Includes a glossary and references for additional reading. | "Core content classroom."--Cover. | Includes bibliographical references and index. | Summary: "A rocky outpost near Baltimore played a bigger role in the history of the United States than anyone imagined it ever would. After America gained its freedom in 1776, the British were determined not to allow the new nation to trade with its enemy France. Discover the unique role Fort McHenry played during the War of 1812."--Provided by publisher.

Identifiers: LCCN 2016954993 | ISBN 978-1-63440-223-1 (library hardcover) | ISBN 978-1-63440-233-0 (paperback) | ISBN 978-1-63440-243-9 (ebook)

Subjects: LCSH: Fort McHenry (Baltimore, Md.)--History--Juvenile literature. | United States--History--War of 1812--Juvenile literature. | CYAC: Fort McHenry (Baltimore, Md.)--History. | United States--History--War of 1812--History.

Classification: LCC E356.B2 M38 2017 (print) | LCC E356.B2 (ebook) | DDC 975.2/6--dc22

Map illustrations by Joe LeMonnier

Illustrations on p. 17, 21 by Laura Jacobsen

Photo credits: p. 17: Courtesy of the Maryland Historical Society; p. 9, 14: Dreamstime; p. 15, 19, 22: Granger; p. 26: Greg Pease, courtesy of Friends of Fort McHenry; p. 25: Historic American Sheet Music, David M. Rubenstein Rare Book & Manuscript Library, Duke University; p. 7, 8, 11, 13, 14, 20, 23, 24: Library of Congress; p. 17: Maryland Historical Society; cover, p. 1, 3, 16, 21, 27, 28, 29, back cover: National Park Service; p. 5: Shutterstock

Printed in the United States of America
0517 1P WRZF17

Table of Contents

The Banner Still Waves!

The United States flag is a powerful symbol of our nation. During a battle, soldiers and others often look to the flag to make sure it is still waving and that the nation it represents has not been defeated. If a flag flying on a fort comes down, the people watching know that the battle has ended in defeat.

Perhaps no one watched the American flag as closely as Francis Scott Key did on September 13, 1814, near Baltimore, Maryland. At that time, the United States was fighting a war against Great Britain. The British had already burned the capital of Washington, D.C., including the White House. Now it looked like they might take control of the city of Baltimore as well.

As Key watched, he strained to see if the American flag still flew over Fort McHenry, just outside the city. It was hard to see through all the smoke and rocket fire. Key peered through a telescope. The flag was still flying! Key was so excited, he wrote a poem about this great event. Later, the poem was set to music. Still later, the song became the **national anthem** of the United States.

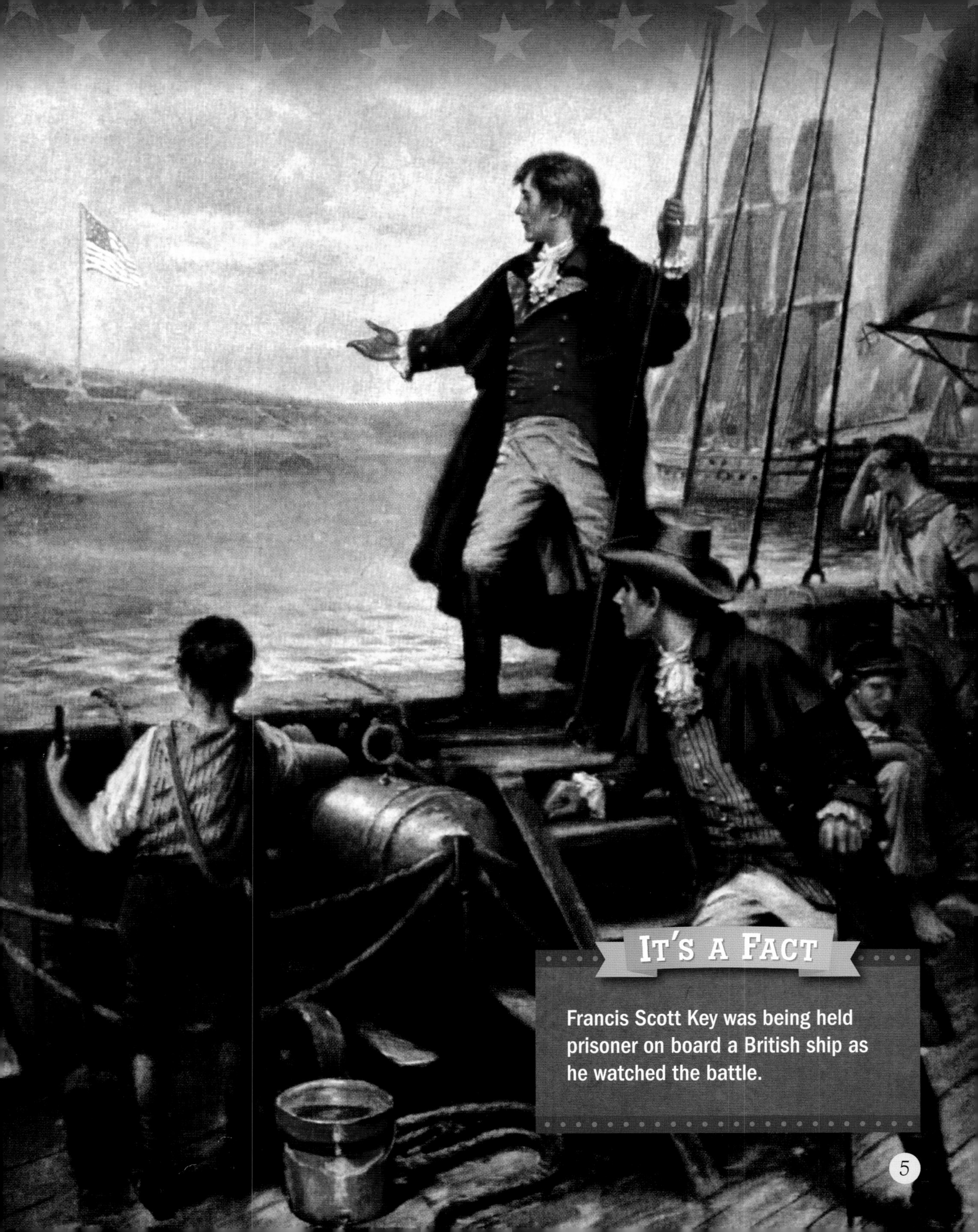

It's a Fact

Francis Scott Key was being held prisoner on board a British ship as he watched the battle.

A New Fort

Between 1776 and 1783, the United States fought a war with Great Britain. The United States had been a colony of Great Britain for many years. However, the colonists were angry about unfair taxes and other laws the British made them follow. They fought a war and won their independence.

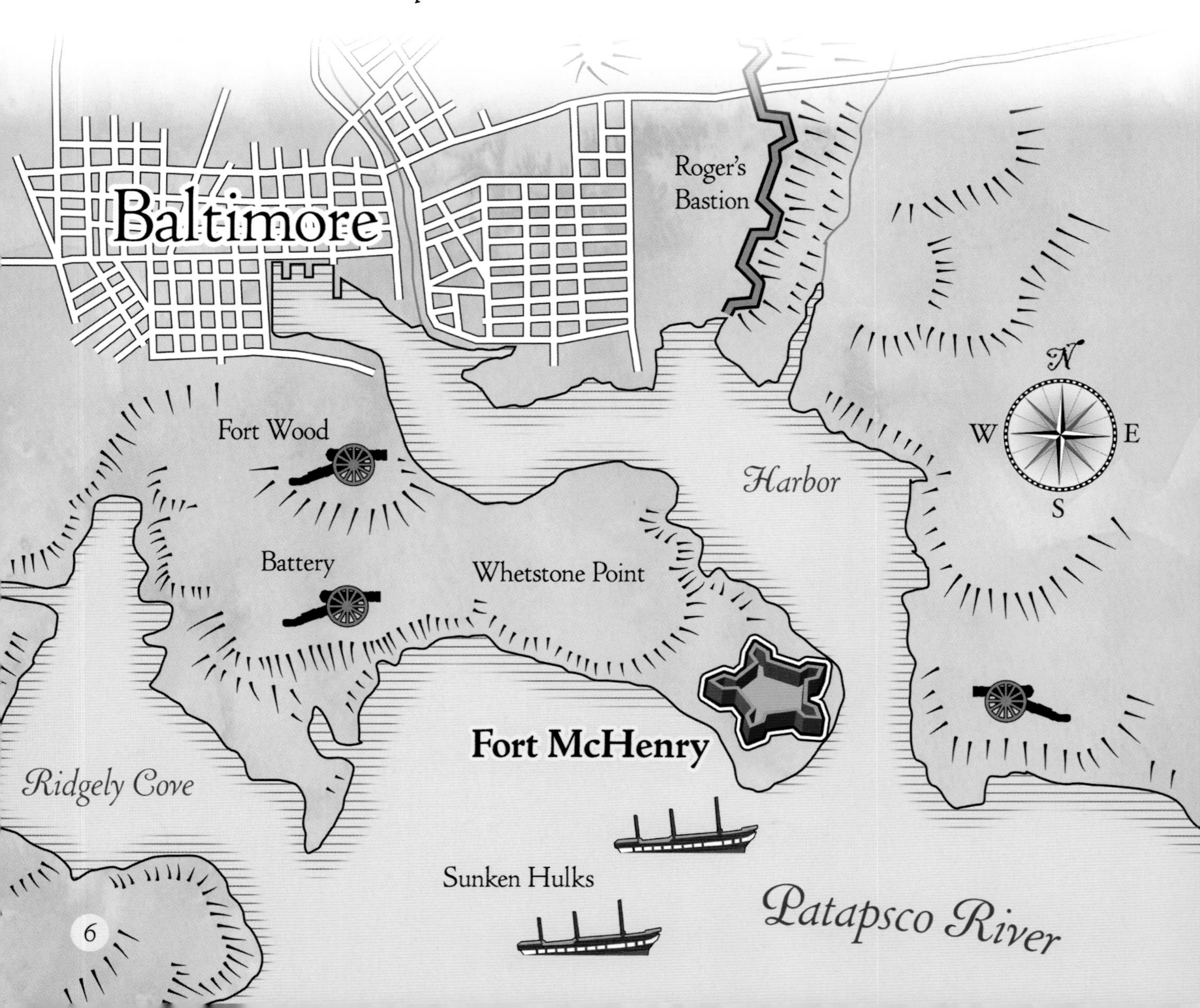

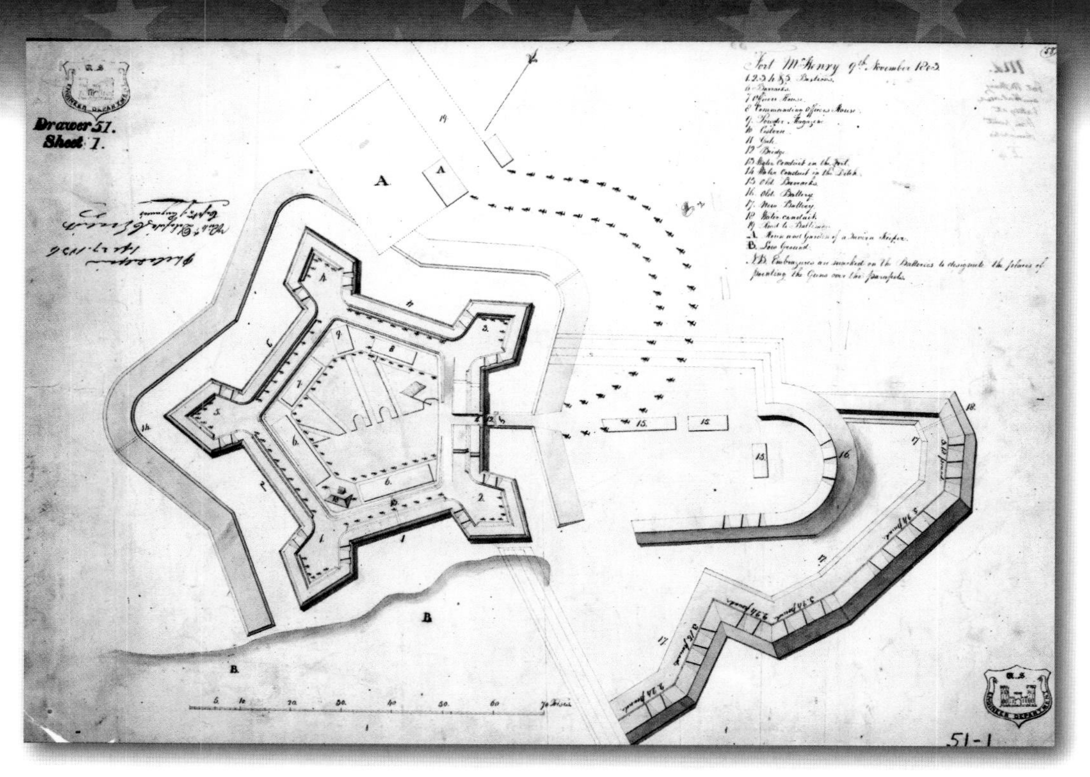

Drawing of Fort McHenry from 1803

The United States knew it might fight another war someday. The new nation wanted to protect its land along the coast of the Atlantic Ocean. In 1794, the government decided to build a string of forts along the coast. Baltimore was an important coastal city, so it was decided to build a fort there.

In 1798, workers began building a new fort. They chose the site of an old fort called Fort Whetstone. The new fort was much bigger and stronger than the old fort. It had five sides and was shaped like a star. At each corner, the walls formed an arrow-shaped point. In 1802, the first troops arrived at the new fort.

Who Was McHenry?

The new fort was named Fort McHenry. It was named after American **patriot** James McHenry. James McHenry was born in Ireland in 1753. In 1771, when he was 18, he moved to Philadelphia to study medicine. McHenry soon became caught up in the American fight for independence. During the Revolution, he served as a **military** surgeon. Later he was captured by the British, but was released. After that, he became a secretary to General George Washington while his American army was stationed at Valley Forge.

James McHenry

Late in the war, McHenry left medicine and began a political career. He became a Maryland State Senator and also served as Secretary of War under Washington and the second president, John Adams.

Since his position put him in charge of the U.S. military, McHenry hired the men who designed the new fort in Baltimore. To honor him, the fort was named after him. McHenry died in Baltimore on May 3, 1816.

It's a Fact

In 1787, McHenry attended the convention that wrote the U.S. Constitution.

Trouble at Sea

Troubles between the United States and Great Britain did not end after the American Revolution. After the war, the U.S. made money by trading goods with countries in Europe. Ships carrying these goods were often boarded by British soldiers. The British were looking for sailors who had deserted, or left, the British Navy. They had the right to capture any deserters they found on U.S. ships. However, the British sometimes took U.S. citizens and made them serve on British ships. This practice was called **impressment**.

The British also wanted to stop the United States from trading with France. During the early 1800s, Great Britain and France were at war, so Great Britain did not want France to receive any goods from other countries. These actions hurt U.S. trade and the young nation's **economy**. Both impressment and restriction of trade made people in the United States very angry.

IT'S A FACT

In 1807, the captain of the USS *Chesapeake* refused to let a British captain board his ship. The British ship fired on the *Chesapeake*, killing three sailors. This incident angered many Americans.

Drawing of the *USS Chesapeake*

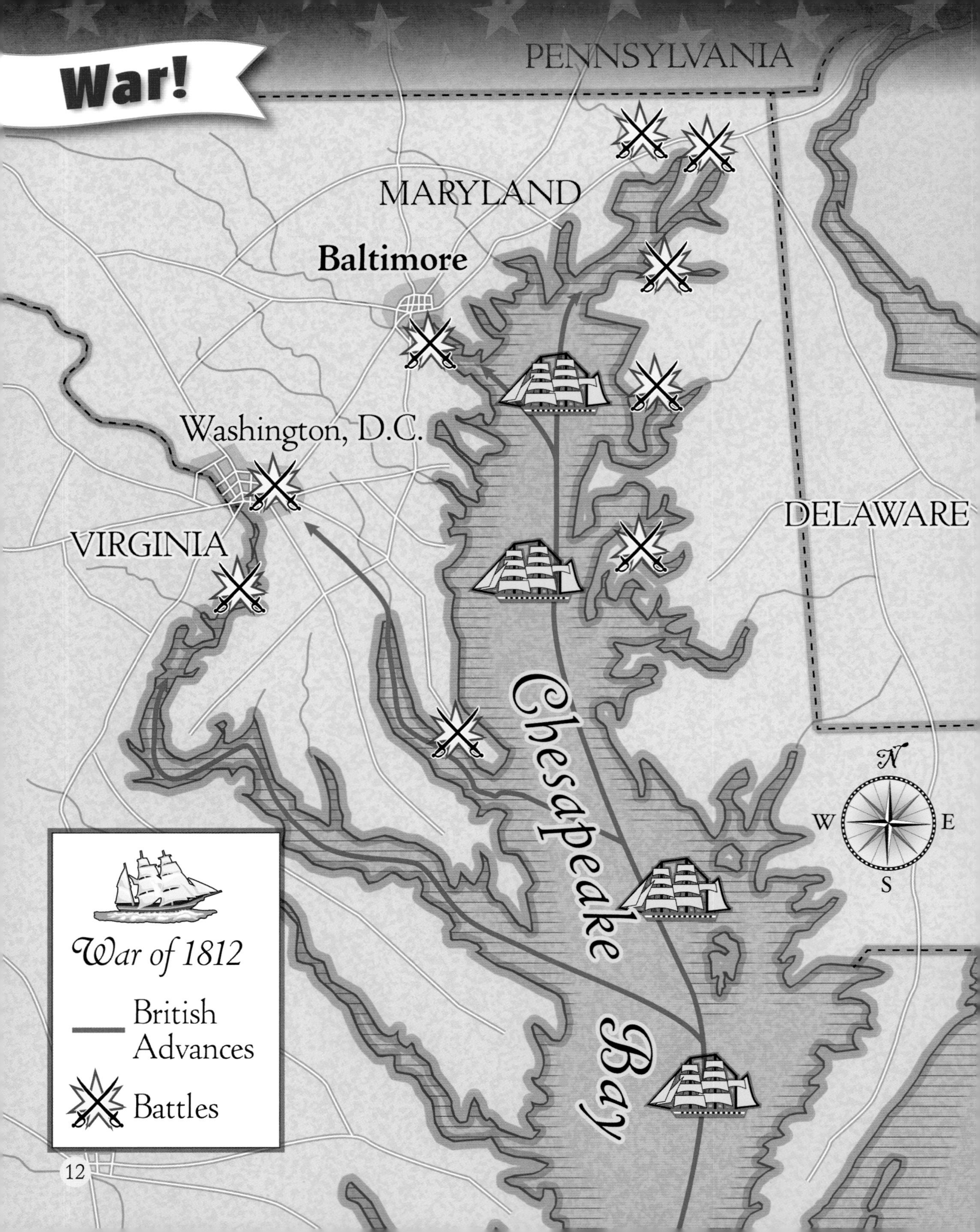
War!
PENNSYLVANIA
MARYLAND
Baltimore
Washington, D.C.
VIRGINIA
DELAWARE
Chesapeake Bay
N
W
E
S
War of 1812
British Advances
Battles

President James Madison

By 1811, some people in the U.S. government wanted to go to war with Great Britain. Finally, in June 1812, President James Madison asked Congress to declare war. Madison said that the United States could not trade freely because of the British attacks and impressments. Congress agreed that Americans had to defend their rights. The U.S. declared war on Great Britain on June 18, 1812.

At first, the war of 1812 went badly for the Americans. The United States only had three large warships, while Great Britain had the most powerful navy in the world. The U.S. also did not have an army of trained soldiers. The British won several major battles around the Great Lakes.

In 1814, the British decided to attack the Atlantic coast. They sailed into Chesapeake Bay in August 1814. The cities of Washington D.C. and Baltimore were two of their targets.

Attack on the White House

British Admiral George Cockburn was eager to attack Washington, D.C. He believed that destroying the nation's capital would make the Americans afraid to fight anymore. On August 19, about 4,000 British troops landed in Maryland. They marched toward Washington, D.C. Along the way, they defeated an American army **battalion**. As the British got closer to Washington, the people who lived in the city ran away. Even President Madison had to leave.

It's a Fact

President Madison's wife, Dolley, managed to save a painting of George Washington that was hanging in the White House. She also took important papers and other items as she left.

The burning of the Capitol by the British

When the British entered the city, they set to work destroying as much as they could. They set fire to all the major public buildings, including the Capitol. Then the British entered the President's House. The building we now call the *White House* was empty. Soldiers sat down and enjoyed a dinner that had been left on the dining room table. Then they set fire to the President's House and left the city.

The Peacemaker at War

When James Madison was only 36-years-old, he wrote the U.S. Bill of Rights so people would have a written plan for protecting their freedoms. As Secretary of State under President Thomas Jefferson, Madison worked closely to build relations with other countries. Yet when British troops attacked American ships, Madison had had enough. The War of 1812 lasted about two years. In the end, Madison was seen as a popular President who stood strong against being bullied by the British.

On to Baltimore

Reenactment of cannon firing at Fort McHenry

After they burned Washington, D.C., the British turned toward the city of Baltimore. Although there were other small forts around the city, everyone knew that Fort McHenry was the most important **defense** of the city. Major George Armistead was in charge of the fort. He commanded about 1,000 soldiers. Fort McHenry also had more than 50 pieces of **artillery**.

Armistead's men kept busy as they waited for the British to arrive. They trained every day. They marched and practiced firing their guns and the fort's cannons. Meanwhile, the British sailed toward the city. They were eager to attack because ships from Baltimore often attacked British supply ships. Some British officers called Baltimore "a nest of pirates."

Major Armistead

On September 12, 1814, the British arrived in Baltimore. Warships sailed into the harbor while about 4,700 troops came on shore. American and British troops fired at each other all through the night. Finally, the Americans **retreated**.

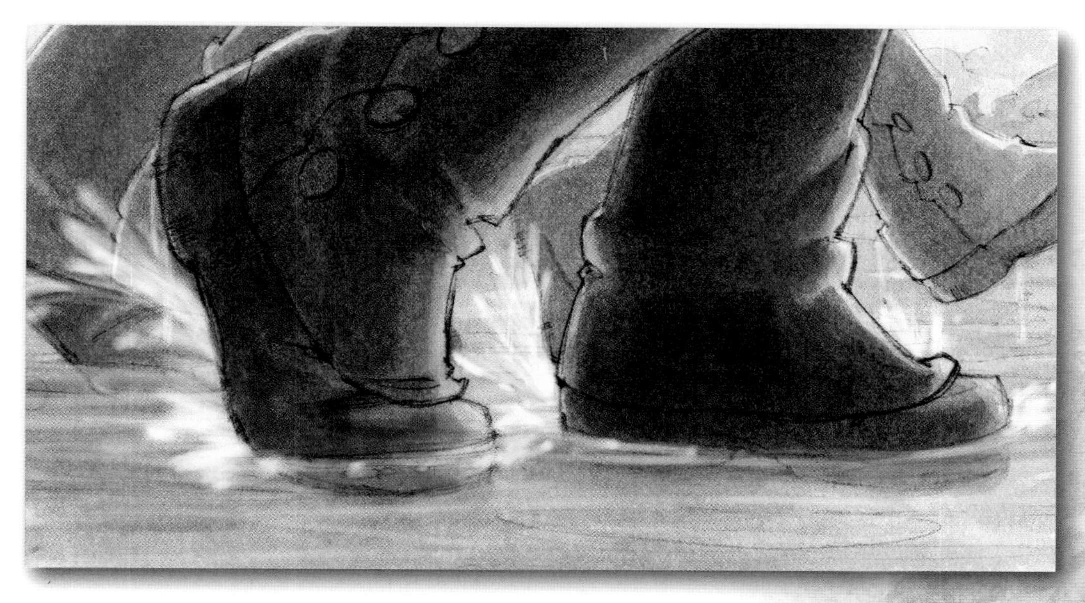

Attack on the Fort

The British began firing on Fort McHenry from their ships on the morning of September 13. Armistead ordered his men to fire back. After a cannonball from Fort McHenry tore through the sail of a British ship, the British moved their ships out of range. Their guns and rockets could still hit the fort, but they did not do much damage.

Armistead told his men to stop firing because he knew the fort's guns could not reach the British ships. The British thought the Americans were ready to give up, so they sailed closer. The Americans opened fire, hitting several British ships. The British moved back again, but they continued firing on the fort as darkness fell.

The British are Coming, Again

By early 1814 the British had won victories in Europe over Napoleon's army. The victory over France freed up dozens of British warships and thousands of troops to cross the Atlantic to take revenge on the Americans for declaring war in 1812 while Britain was already in a war with France. British commander Lord Eglinton declared, "The only thing now is those cursed Americans. I hope a sufficient force will be sent to crush them at once, to attack their strongholds, arsenals, shipping, and naval yards, and destroy them."

The British naval bombardment of Fort McHenry

During the night of September 13, the British tried to sneak troops into Baltimore by boat. Watching from a ship in the harbor, Francis Scott Key described what happened next:

"Fort McHenry opened the full force of all her guns upon them...and the fleet responding with entire broadsides made an explosion so terrific...the heavens aglow were a seething sea of flame, and the waters of the harbor were lashed into an angry sea by the vibrations..."

Francis Scott Key

Francis Scott Key

Francis Scott Key was an American officer at the time of the attack on Fort McHenry. A week before the battle, he and another American, John Skinner, boarded a British ship. President Madison had asked them to gain the release of an American doctor named William Beanes. Beanes had been captured during the attack on Washington, D.C. The British agreed to let Beanes leave the ship with the Americans. However, when the British decided to attack Baltimore, they refused to let any of the Americans leave the ship, which was about eight miles from the fort. The British did not want the Americans to tell anyone that the British planned to attack.

Stuck onboard the ship, Key had a good view of the battle. He used a telescope to watch the fort and make sure the American flag was still flying. Then it began to rain and night fell. The British stopped firing, but Key could not see the fort or the flag in the darkness. All night he wondered, "Was the American flag still flying?"

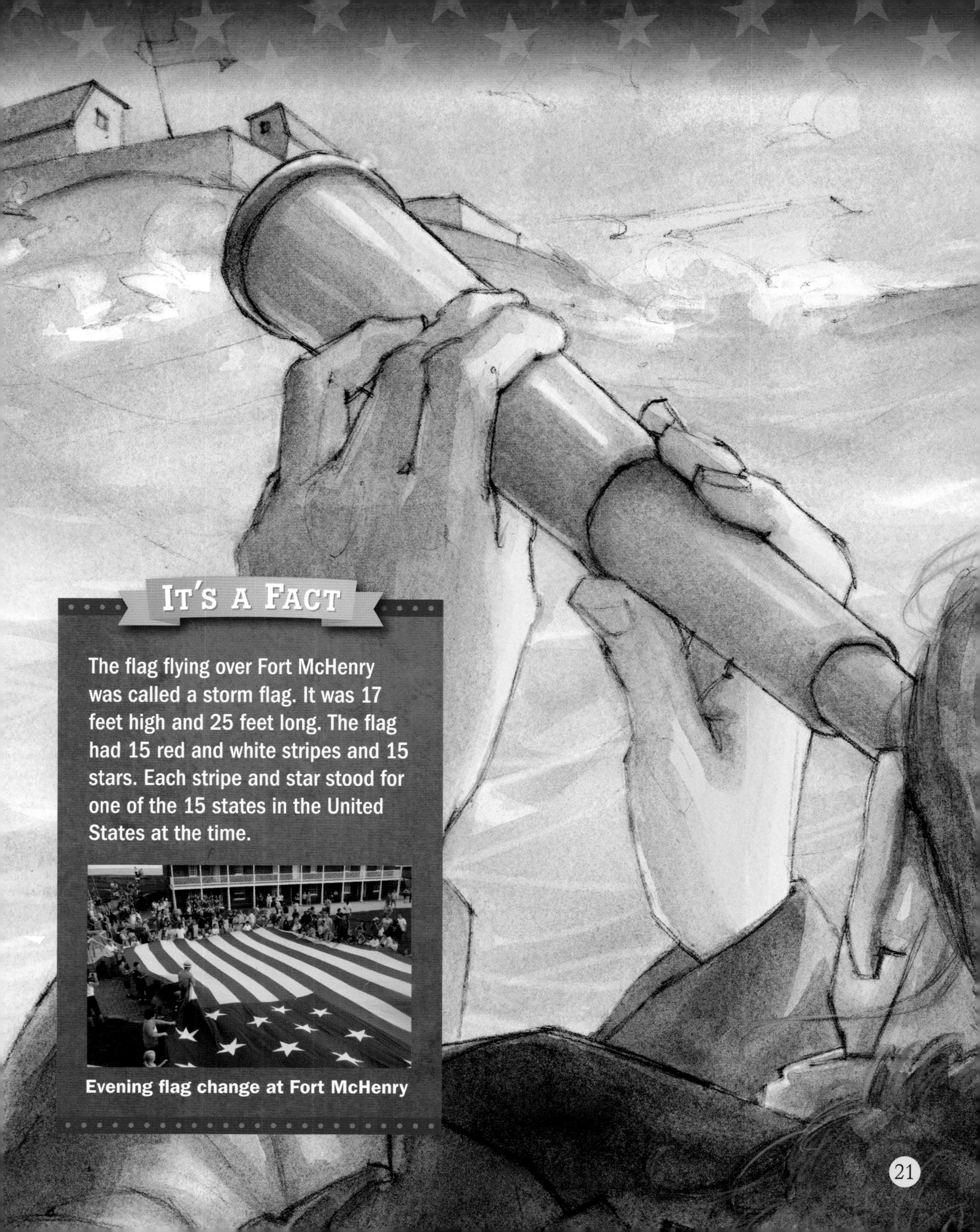

It's a Fact

The flag flying over Fort McHenry was called a storm flag. It was 17 feet high and 25 feet long. The flag had 15 red and white stripes and 15 stars. Each stripe and star stood for one of the 15 states in the United States at the time.

Evening flag change at Fort McHenry

Finally, the sun rose on a new day. Everything was quiet. No shots were fired. Key looked at the fort and wondered what he would see. He was greeted by a wonderful sight. Major Armistead had taken down the storm flag and put up an even bigger flag. Fort McHenry was safe! The battle was over! The British ships left the harbor without attacking the city.

When Key got back on land, he wrote a poem describing the battle and what it was like to watch the flag waving in the middle of the fighting. A friend published the poem and handed it out to people in Baltimore. He called the poem "The Defense of Fort McHenry." However, Key later came up with a better title. He called it "The Star-Spangled Banner."

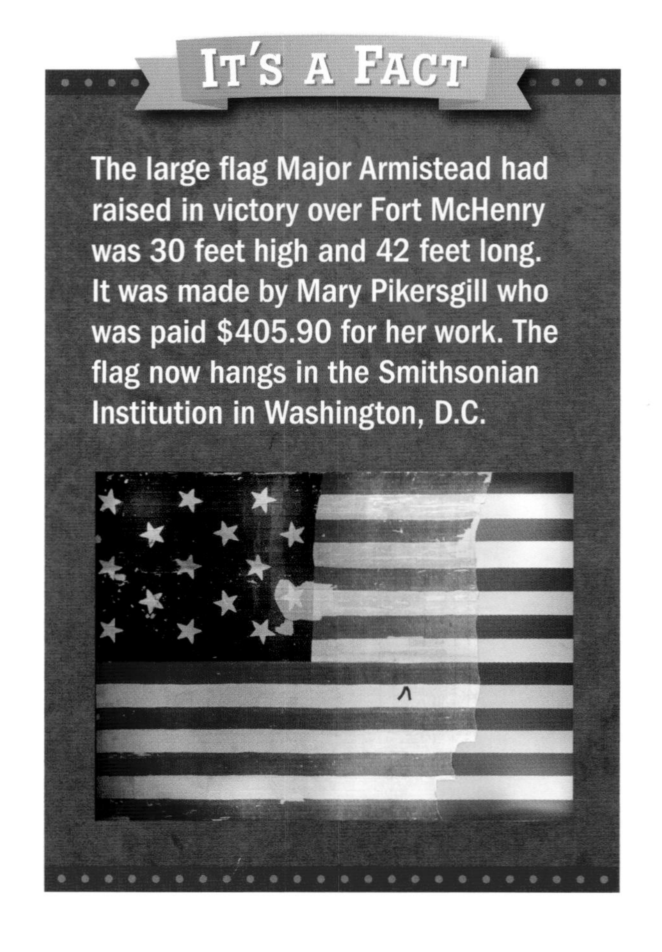

It's a Fact

The large flag Major Armistead had raised in victory over Fort McHenry was 30 feet high and 42 feet long. It was made by Mary Pikersgill who was paid $405.90 for her work. The flag now hangs in the Smithsonian Institution in Washington, D.C.

O say can you see ~~through~~ by the dawn's early light
What so proudly we hail'd at the twilight's last gleaming,
Whose broad stripes & bright stars through the perilous fight
O'er the ramparts we watch'd, were so gallantly streaming?
And the rocket's red glare, the bomb bursting in air,
Gave proof through the night that our flag was still there,
O say does that star-spangled banner yet wave
O'er the land of the free & the home of the brave?

On the shore dimly seen through the mists of the deep,
Where the foe's haughty host in dread silence reposes,
What is that which the breeze, o'er the towering steep,
As it fitfully blows, half conceals, half discloses?
Now it catches the gleam of the morning's first beam,
In full glory reflected now shines on the stream,
'Tis the star-spangled banner — O long may it wave
O'er the land of the free & the home of the brave!

And where is that band who so vauntingly swore,
That the havoc of war & the battle's confusion
A home & a Country should leave us no more?
— ~~[illegible]~~
Their blood has wash'd out their foul footstep's pollution.
No refuge could save the hireling & slave
From the terror of flight or the gloom of the grave,
And the star-spangled banner in triumph doth wave
O'er the land of the free & the home of the brave.

O thus be it ever when freemen shall stand
Between their lov'd home & the war's desolation!
Blest with vict'ry & peace may the heav'n rescued land
Praise the power that hath made & preserv'd us a nation!
Then conquer we must, when our cause it is just,
And this be our motto — "In God is our trust,"
And the star-spangled banner in triumph shall wave
O'er the land of the free & the home of the brave. —

Original manuscript of "The Star-Spangled Banner" by Francis Scott Key

America's Anthem

People loved Key's poem and its thrilling story. They began singing it to the tune of a popular song called "To Anacreon in Heaven." Newspapers also printed the poem. People all over the country learned the words and enjoyed its story of the American **victory**.

"The Star-Spangled Banner" remained popular for the next hundred years. Soldiers fighting in the Civil War from 1861-1865 sang it. Army and Navy bands played it at ceremonies. In time, people all over the world heard the song. It became a symbol of America.

In 1919, President Woodrow Wilson ordered that "The Star-Spangled Banner" be played at all official government events. Finally, on March 3, 1931, Congress declared "The Star-Spangled Banner" to be the official national anthem of the United States. President Herbert Hoover signed the bill and the U.S. finally had a song to call its own.

President Herbert Hoover

3
THE STAR SPANGLED BANNER.
Maestoso.
PIANO.
2. On the shore dim - ly seen thro' the mists of the deep, Where the
1. O say can you see by the dawn's ear - ly light, What so
foe's haughty host in dread silence re - po - ses, What is that which the breeze, o'er the
proudly we hail'd at the twilight's last gleaming, Whose broad stripes and bright stars thro' the
tow - er - ing steep, As it fit - ful - ly blows, half con-ceals, ha
per - il - ous fight, O'er the ramparts we watch'd were so gal-lan
G. A & Co.
STAR SPANGLED BANNER.
TRANSCRIBED FOR THE PIANO,
by
Ch. Voss.
G. ANDRE & CO.
1104 Chestnut St. Philad.

Fort McHenry After the War

The War of 1812 officially ended in February 1815 with a U.S. victory. President Madison knew that coastal forts were important. He ordered workers to add stronger walls at Fort McHenry. Later, in 1829, more improvements were made. Workers added new guns and walls. They also added a second floor to the buildings inside.

Between 1846 and 1848, America fought a war against Mexico. American troops trained at Fort McHenry. During the Civil War, Fort McHenry was used as a prison for Confederate soldiers. This was the last time the fort would be used as it was originally intended or even as a prison.

It's a Fact

In 2014, Fort McHenry held a Living Flag ceremony. More than 6,600 schoolchildren from across Maryland dressed in red, white, and blue to make up the flag. Living Flag programs are still held at Fort McHenry.

Aerial view of Fort McHenry today

After the Civil War, Fort McHenry was only used as a base for troops. Because the United States built a powerful navy, it no longer needed coastal forts to protect its land. Later the fort was a public park. During World War I, it became a military hospital. The fort also served as a training base and lookout point during World War II.

A National Shrine

In 1925, the U.S. government named Fort McHenry a national park. After some work was done to the buildings, the fort opened to the public in 1928. In 1939, the fort was honored again. The government announced that Fort McHenry was a national **monument** and a national shrine. It is the only national monument and **shrine** in the U.S. national park system.

An air show at Fort McHenry

Guard drummers and flag

More than 600,000 people visit Fort McHenry every year. Visitors can watch a short film in the Visitor Center and see exhibits describing the British attack and the battle that inspired Francis Scott Key. They can also learn about the fort's different American flags and their history. Of course, visitors can tour the fort itself. The tour includes **barracks** where soldiers lived, storage areas, cannons and other artillery.

Many special events are held at Fort McHenry. People dress in old uniforms to show visitors what life was like at the fort during the war of 1812. There are concerts and parades. On Memorial Day, the fort flies historic U.S. flags to honor those who gave their lives during wars.

Glossary

artillery: cannons and other large guns

barracks: buildings where soldiers live and sleep

battalion: a military unit of several hundred soldiers

defense: the act of defending against an attack

economy: the wealth and resources of a country

impressment: forcing someone into military duty

military: having to do with the armed forces

monument: a statue or building erected to honor a historical person or event

national anthem: the official song of a nation

patriot: someone who is loyal to his or her country

retreated: moved back; withdrew from battle

shrine: a place that is considered special because of events that took place there

victory: the act of defeating an enemy

Learn More in the Library

Books

Kroll, Steven. *By the Dawn's Early Light.* Scholastic, 2000.

Kulling, Monica. *Francis Scott Key's Star Spangled Banner* (Step Into Reading). Random House Children's Books, 2012.

Miklos, Jr., John. *A Primary Source History of The War of 1812*. Capstone Press, 2016.

Welch, Catherine A. *The Star-Spangled Banner* (On My Own History). Millbrook Press, 2005.

Web Sites

National Park Service: Ft. McHenry

www.nps.gov/fomc/index.htm

Smithsonian: The Star-Spangled Banner

http://amhistory.si.edu/starspangledbanner/default.aspx

Index